by Harry Conroy

Lang**Syne**

PUBLISHING

WRITING *to* REMEMBER

LangSyne

PUBLISHING

WRITING *to* REMEMBER

79 Main Street, Newtongrange,
Midlothian EH22 4NA
Tel: 0131 344 0414   Fax: 0845 075 6085
E-mail: info@lang-syne.co.uk
www.langsyneshop.co.uk

Design by Dorothy Meikle
Printed by Printwell Ltd
© Lang Syne Publishers Ltd 2016

ISBN 978-1-85217-103-2

Scott

SEPT NAMES INCLUDE

Laidlaw
Langlands
Hardin
Geddes
Buccleuch
Balwearie

Scott

MOTTO:
Amo (I Love).

CREST:
A stag trippant Proper
attired and unguled Or.

TERRITORY:
Teviotdale, Ewesdale,
Eskdale and Liddesdale.

Chapter one:

The origins of the clan system

by Rennie McOwan

The original Scottish clans of the Highlands and the great families of the Lowlands and Borders were gatherings of families, relatives, allies and neighbours for mutual protection against rivals or invaders.

Scotland experienced invasion from the Vikings, the Romans and English armies from the south. The Norman invasion of what is now England also had an influence on land-holding in Scotland. Some of these invaders stayed on and in time became 'Scottish'.

The word clan derives from the Gaelic language term 'clann', meaning children, and it was first used many centuries ago as communities were formed around tribal lands in glens and mountain fastnesses.

The format of clans changed over the centuries, but at its best the chief and his family held the land on behalf of all, like trustees, and the ordinary clansmen and women believed they had a blood relationship with the founder of their clan.

There were two way duties and obligations. An inadequate chief could be deposed and replaced by someone of greater ability.

Clan people had an immense pride in race. Their relationship with the chief was like adult children to a father and they had a real dignity.

The concept of clanship is very old and a more feudal notion of authority gradually crept in.

Pictland, for instance, was divided into seven principalities ruled by feudal leaders who were the strongest and most charismatic leaders of their particular groups.

By the sixth century the 'British' kingdoms of Strathclyde, Lothian and Celtic Dalriada (Argyll) had emerged and Scotland, as one nation, began to take shape in the time of King Kenneth MacAlpin.

Some chiefs claimed descent from

ancient kings which may not have been accurate in every case.

By the twelfth and thirteenth centuries the clans and families were more strongly brought under the central control of Scottish monarchs.

Lands were awarded and administered more and more under royal favour, yet the power of the area clan chiefs was still very great.

The long wars to ensure Scotland's independence against the expansionist ideas of English monarchs extended the influence of some clans and reduced the lands of others.

Those who supported Scotland's greatest king, Robert the Bruce, were awarded the territories of the families who had opposed his claim to the Scottish throne.

In the Scottish Borders country – the notorious Debatable Lands – the great families built up a ferocious reputation for providing warlike men accustomed to raiding into England and occasionally fighting one another.

Chiefs had the power to dispense justice and to confiscate lands and clan warfare produced a society where martial virtues – courage, hardiness, tenacity – were greatly admired.

Gradually the relationship between the clans and the Crown became strained as Scottish monarchs became more orientated to life in the Lowlands and, on occasion, towards England.

The Highland clans spoke a different language, Gaelic, whereas the language of Lowland Scotland and the court was Scots and in more modern times, English.

Highlanders dressed differently, had different customs, and their wild mountain land sometimes seemed almost foreign to people living in the Lowlands.

It must be emphasised that Gaelic culture was very rich and story-telling, poetry, piping, the clarsach (harp) and other music all flourished and were greatly respected.

Highland culture was different from other parts of Scotland but it was not inferior or less sophisticated.

Central Government, whether in London or Edinburgh, sometimes saw the Gaelic clans as

*"The spirit of the clan means much
to thousands of people"*

a challenge to their authority and some sent expeditions into the Highlands and west to crush the power of the Lords of the Isles.

Nevertheless, when the eighteenth century Jacobite Risings came along the cause of the Stuarts was mainly supported by Highland clans.

The word Jacobite comes from the Latin for James – Jacobus. The Jacobites wanted to restore the exiled Stuarts to the throne of Britain.

The monarchies of Scotland and England became one in 1603 when King James VI of Scotland (1st of England) gained the English throne after Queen Elizabeth died.

The Union of Parliaments of Scotland and England, the Treaty of Union, took place in 1707.

Some Highland clans, of course, and Lowland families opposed the Jacobites and supported the incoming Hanoverians.

After the Jacobite cause finally went down at Culloden in 1746 a kind of ethnic cleansing took place. The power of the chiefs was curtailed. Tartan and the pipes were banned in law.

Many emigrated, some because they

wanted to, some because they were evicted by force. In addition, many Highlanders left for the cities of the south to seek work.

Many of the clan lands became home to sheep and deer shooting estates.

But the warlike traditions of the clans and the great Lowland and Border families lived on, with their descendants fighting bravely for freedom in two world wars.

Remember the men from whence you came, says the Gaelic proverb, and to that could be added the role of many heroic women.

The spirit of the clan, of having roots, whether Highland or Lowland, means much to thousands of people.

*Clan warfare produced a society where
courage and tenacity were greatly admired*

Chapter two:

A powerful clan

The Clan Scott was one of the most powerful border clans and members of the clan could be found across large swathes of the Border hills.

The heart of Scott country was Bellendain, but they were also to be found in West Teviotdale, Ewesdale, Eskdale and Liddesdale, around Hawick, Selkirk and Melrose in the district of Roxburgh-shire.

They preferred being called Borderers to Lowlanders, although their lands are in the Scottish Lowlands.

The Latin word Scotti originally referred to the Irish Celts, then later Gaels in general. However the earliest record of the name Scott was attributed to Uchtred Filius Scott who witnessed a charter around 1120.

Uchtred was said to have had two sons, Richard and Michael. From Richard eventually grew the family branch known as the Scots of

Buccleuch, and from Michael came the Scotts of Balweary.

Four generations later Uchtred's descendent, Sir Richard Scott, began his family's transformation into peaceful landowners when he married Alicia, daughter of Henry of Molla and heiress of Murthockstone, thereby acquiring her estates.

Sir Richard was appointed Ranger of Ettrick Forest, which added the lands of Rankilburn to his properties. He built his family residence at Buccleuch and thereafter the estates went by the name of Buccleuch.

Uchtred's second son, Michael, married Margaret, daughter of Duncan Syras of Syras, and gained the lands of Ceres. They had one child, Duncan, who in turn had two children, Michael and Gilbert.

Michael was knighted by Alexander II and married Margaret Balwearie, daughter and sole heiress of Sir Richard Balwearie. The marriage brought to Michael the lands of Balwearie in the parish of Abbotshall.

Sir Michael was an ardent supporter of Robert the Bruce and later of King David II.

He met his death in 1346 fighting at Durham and he left two sons, Robert and John, who between them founded the two great branches of the Scott clan. The eldest, Robert, inherited the Buccleuch and Murdochston estates, to which he added Scotstoun, while John founded the cadet house of Synton, from which the Lords of Polworth are descended.

Thus began the two great branches of the Scott clan.

Robert the Bruce – Kings of Scots

Chapter three:

Sworn enemies

By the dawn of the sixteenth century there was acrimony between the Scotts and their neighbours, the Kerrs.

This gathered momentum when Sir Walter Scott of Buccleuch took it upon himself to attempt to free James V from the clutches of the Earl of Angus. The young king was being held captive at Darnick which lies to the west of the town of Melrose.

Scott launched his attack on July 25, 1526, and Kerr of Cessford was slain during the battle. Sir Walter was also wounded but recovered and went on to fight at the battle of Pinkie in 1547. Later he was appointed as warden of Liddesdale and the Middle Marches.

The Kerrs however had not forgiven their sworn enemy for the death of Kerr of Cessford. A chance meeting in Edinburgh's High Street on October 4, 1552 between a number of the Kerr clan and Sir Walter led to the Scott chief being slain.

The feuding finally came to an end when Sir Thomas of Ferniehirst married Janet Scott, the sister of the 10th Laird of Buccleuch. The Laird was an ardent supporter of Mary, Queen of Scots until he died, leaving his son, also named Walter after his illustrious ancestors, to inherit his estates while still very young.

This Walter was very much in the mould of his predecessors. He was born in 1565 and succeeded his father in 1574. He went on to become a renowned military leader that history remembers as the Bold Buccleuch. He was involved in every Border raid of his time, and was held in Blackness for a skirmish in which he played a leading part, but he escaped and received letters of pardon from King James VI on March 3, 1582-83.

His imprisonment seems not to have taught the Bold Buccleuch any lessons. Following his release he took part in a raid against England in 1587 and was promptly imprisoned again, this time in Edinburgh Castle, but released fairly quickly.

A more serious problem for the King was Sir Walter's acceptance of the turbulent antics of the Earl of Bothwell, who had married his mother on the death of his father. He complied with his stepfather's lawlessness to the extent that he was banished to France for three years.

However he sought a pardon in 1592 and was permitted to return to Scotland in November of that year.

Meanwhile, the King had run out of patience with the Earl of Bothwell and confiscated his lands, giving them to the Duke of Lennox who was a firm favourite at the time.

The Duke, in turn, held the lands for three years before returning them to the King, who immediately conferred the Bothwell estates on Sir Walter as a reward for helping to bring peace to the Borders.

The same Sir Walter, however, had participated in many raids, while supposedly helping to maintain law and order. He actively took the law into his own hands when he considered that any of his supporters had suffered at the hands of English freebooters.

One of his better known exploits was the rescuing of his staunch supporter, William Armstrong, otherwise known as Kinmount Willie, from the previously impenetrable fortress of Carlisle Castle.

During this time, the Scotts were at their most powerful. They could call upon large numbers of followers and as many as 600 would follow them into battle, or take part in a raid organised by Sir Walter.

However, after the union of the Crowns in 1603, cross-border raids came to an end as it was no longer tolerable to have border warfare continuing in what was supposed to be a United Kingdom.

When relative peace was brought to the area many clansmen went to fight in Holland as members of the Scots brigade.

Sir Walter was appointed commander of a body of troops under Prince Maurice of the Netherlands in 1604, where he served until a truce was called in 1609.

In 1606 he had been created a Lord of Parliament in Scotland and was given the title Lord Scott of Buccleuch, and appointed a member of the Privy Council on February 26, 1611.

Such positions in the London establishment transformed the clan chiefs. They became great noblemen, leaders of powerful families rather than adhering to the old clan system of their ancestors.

Sir Walter, or Lord Scott as he was then, died on December 15, 1611 at Branksholm, aged 46, and was buried at Hawick. He left a son and three daughters, his wife having been a daughter of Sir William Kerr of Cessford, the erstwhile enemy of his house.

His son, another Walter, was the first for over 140 years to inherit the Buccleuch estates after having reached majority. He was a military man like his father, who commanded a regiment for the States of Holland against the Spanish. He was given the title of Earl of Buccleuch in 1619. He spent his entire life in the service of his country, and was in active service until six weeks before his death in November 1633.

Chapter four:

The young Countess

Walter's successor, his second son, Francis, the second Earl of Buccleuch, supported the National Covenant and was against attempts by Charles I to introduce the English form of religion into Scotland.

The second Earl was known to be not only a brave but a very pious man greatly drawn to his religion. In 1645 he led his men against Montrose at Philipshaugh. This victory by the Covenanters marked the turning point in the King's war in Scotland. Buccleuch died in 1651, at the age of 25.

He was succeeded by his daughter Mary, who was just four years old. Her title was Countess of Buccleuch.

Unfortunately for the young Countess, her mother, Lady Margaret Leslie, widow of Lord Balgonie, whom Earl Francis had married at the age of twenty, was a selfish, greedy, unscrupulous and self serving woman. Upon the death of the gentle Earl, Lady Margaret rapidly found herself another husband in the form of the second Earl of Wemyss.

The child Countess was the subject of many plots. Her tutors set about marrying the child off to their own advantage, coming up with many and varied suitors, but were thwarted in all their attempts by the young girl's mother, who had other (just as dishonourable) plans of her own for the hapless child.

Lady Margaret, along with her uncle the Duke of Rothess and Sir Gideon Scott of Highchester, plotted to arrange a marriage for the young Countess to one of Sir Gideon's young sons, the children being respectively eleven and fourteen years old at the time.

The marriage was illegally performed without the proclamation of banns, care being taken to make sure the marriage contract bestowed on the young husband the life rent of the honours and estates of the Earldom whilst paying the Countess's mother and stepfather very handsomely for having the young bride stay with them until she was eighteen.

The children were separated when the plot was uncovered by Earl Francis's overseers. The Countess refused to be defeated. Upon reaching the "legal" age of twelve, the arrangement was again ratified at the insistence of Lady Margaret and her cohorts, the children having signed a document of adherence.

Sadly, however, young Countess Mary, who was said to have taken her father's gentle character, succumbed to illness and died before she was fourteen in 1661. Her husband gained nothing from their marriage other than the title for life of Earl of Tarras, having been outwitted by her mother with regard to Mary's last will.

Lady Margaret's scheming ensured that she and her fellow plotters benefited from the estate. They received a huge sum of money, which they divided between them.

On the death of Countess Mary, the Buccleuch titles and estates passed on to her only sister, Lady Anne Scott. Immediately her mother and her unscrupulous brother began to arrange a marriage for the child, who was only eleven at the time.

They wrote to Charles II suggesting that Anne would be a suitable bride for his illegitimate son, James, Duke of Monmouth. Since Anne was one of the most eligible heiresses of her day the offer was readily accepted and they were married in April, 1663.

King Charles created the couple the Duke and Duchess of Buccleuch. They remained at court and the Duchess was known for her prudence and discretion.

Unfortunately the same could not be said of her husband. The Duchess was a dutiful wife, bearing four sons and two daughters, but the Duke was not a faithful husband. He met an inglorious end when, rising in rebellion against the Crown, he was captured, tried and ordered to be executed.

Three years after Monmouth's execution, Anne married again. Her second husband was Charles, third Lord Cornwallis, with whom she was said to be very happy. They had three children, a son and two daughters.

Despite her husband's execution, Anne retained the title Duchess of Buccleuch in her own right. She lived until the ripe old age of 81. Although she died in London on February 6, 1732, her body was buried at Dalkeith.

Her marriage to Monmouth, despite his fall from grace, placed the Scott family on the highest strata of aristocratic society, and succeeding generations divided their time between London and the family estates in Scotland.

Anne was succeeded by her grandson James, who in 1745 called on his tenants to resist Bonnie Prince Charlie's advance on Edinburgh. James was in turn succeeded by his grandson Henry who was only five years old when he became the 3rd Duke of Buccleuch.

Henry was educated at Eton as were most of the Dukes of Buccleuch who followed him. He travelled abroad with Adam Smith, author of *The Wealth of Nations*.

In 1783 Henry became President of the

Royal Society of Scotland, having already been appointed a Knight of the Thistle in 1767.

The 4th Duke of Buccleuch, Charles William Henry Scott, succeeded to the Dukedom in 1812 and was a close friend of the author and poet Sir Walter Scott who was a member of the Scotts of Harden branch of the family.

Sir Walter, who resided at Abbotsford, acknowledged the 5th Duke of Buccleuch as his Clan Chief and patron.

The high station in society held by the Duke of Buccleuch was established beyond doubt when first King George IV in 1822 and then Queen Victoria in 1842 were received at Dalkeith by Walter Francis Scott, the 5th Duke of Buccleuch.

Walter Francis held the position of Lord Privy Seal from 1842 to 1846. This eminent position in society remains until present times. The current Duke of Buccleuch is the tenth. He is also the Duke of Queensberry, a title held by the Duke of Buccleuch since 1810 when the fourth Duke of Queensberry died without issue.

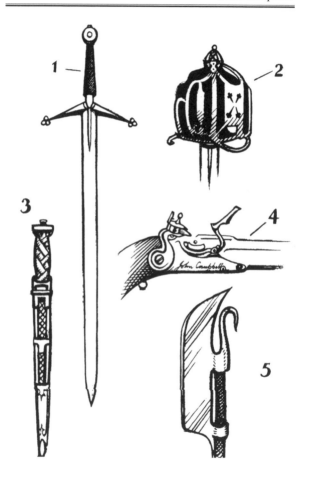

Clan weapons

1)   The claymore or two-handed sword
(fifteenth or early sixteenth century)

2)   Basket hilt of broadsword
made in Stirling, 1716

3)   Highland dirk
(eighteenth century)

4)   Steel pistol *(detail)* made in Doune

5)   Head of Lochaber Axe as carried
in the '45 and earlier